Love *Makes* *The* *Sacrifice*

Healing While Kneeling

James & Tenisia Evans

TABLE OF CONTENTS

CHAPTER ONE 5

Love Lifted Me

Don't Give Away Your Good Thing 6
Although We Were Young, We Had Destiny On Our Side 9
Season... Time... Purpose 11

CHAPTER TWO 13

Separation Anxiety

The High School Years.. 13

CHAPTER THREE 17

Married with Children

CHAPTER FOUR 21

Taming the Tongue

CHAPTER FIVE 25

Socializing and Setting the Example

CHAPTER SIX 31

When Loving You Is Hurting Me

CHAPTER SEVEN 35

The Process of Forgiveness

CHAPTER EIGHT 37

Healing While Kneeling

Pastor Tenisia's Personal Testimony 39
Healing While Kneeling 41

CHAPTER NINE 43

Surviving the Storm

Love Makes the Sacrifice 45

Chapter One

Love Lifted Me

<u>*Ecclesiastes 4:9-12 (NLT)*</u>

Two people can accomplish more than twice as much as one; they get a better return for their labor. If one person falls, the other can reach out and help.

But people who are alone when they fall are in real trouble. And on a cold night, two under the same blanket can gain warmth from each other. But how can one be warm alone?

A person standing alone can be attacked and defeated, but two can stand back-to-back and conquer. Three are even better, for a triple-braided cord is not easily broken.

Don't Give Away Your Good Thing

His

My wife and I met in the fall of 1985 in our freshman year of high school. I had no idea that the day she walked into my classical music class would forever change my destiny. Although she was attractive (cute), I initially tried to "hook her up" with a fellow classmate. My first response to seeing her still resonates with me today, "hey, look at the new girl".

However, it would be her words that forever changed our lives! As I tried to play matchmaker between her and this fellow, she uttered these Prophetic words to me, "I don't want *him*... **I want you!**

It would be these words, uttered by a prophetess yet to be discovered, that would Impact my soul, uplift my spirit and usher me into my Prophesied place in God.

> *1 Thessalonians 5:20-21 (NIV)*
> **Do not treat prophecies with contempt but test them all; hold on to what is good.**

Hers

I recall that day as if it were yesterday, as I entered the room I remembered a young handsome man standing at the door of the class, with a brown brief case in his hands, He was wearing a blue adidas track suit with crispy white top 10 gym shoes. He had a smile that captivated me as he spoke those words "Hey there's a new girl in our class". I knew at that point he would be my husband and I had not even received his number. When I finally began to talk with him on the phone, we would talk for hours. I remember going home and telling my parents, you have got to meet him. He was full of the wisdom of God. So again, I thank God that I decreed and declared that he was mine, and God established this Relationship.

<u>Proverbs 18:22 (ESV)</u>
He who finds a wife finds a good thing
And obtains favor from the Lord.

His

I wish I could say that it was love at first sight, but at fourteen years of age I had no clue what real love was. Quite frankly, my testosterone levels were so high that I was "loving" a whole lot in those days. However, her words indicated to me early on that I was dealing with someone who knew what they wanted. When I heard her "declare" that she wanted me, I initially rejected it. I played the mind games of avoidance that so many of us have entertained throughout our lives. Because I struggled with the spirit of rejection, I couldn't receive from her, that she "wanted" me.

I'm reminded of the story of Mephibosheth, in 2 Samuel 9:8, *"And he bowed himself, and said, What is thy servant, that thou shouldest look upon such a dead dog as I am?" (KJV)*

I thought to myself, if she wants me, there has to be something wrong with her. However, I've learned since then, that this is not your ordinary woman. This is a woman who goes after what she wants.

Hers

I had always been taught God's word according to Psalm 20:4, *"May he give you the desire of your heart and make all your plans succeed." (NIV)* And I knew that God would give me my hearts desire, I was determined, Yes he did play the games of avoidance, giving me the wrong phone number and the wrong name and I must admit, so did I, by playing on his phone. But I admired his wisdom and the ability in my eyes to finally have a friend I could trust. I was able to open up to him and talk to him about things that hurt me and things that had been done to me as a child. He would give me advice and walk me through what I struggled with. I now realize that we were there to strengthen each other.

Although We Were Young, We Had Destiny On Our Side

There was an eight-month gap between our first meeting and our official and exclusive courtship. If you were to ask me what sealed the bond that we share now, I would honestly admit that it wasn't her beauty, of which she has in abundance. It wasn't simply the physical attraction either. What made me fall in love with her was her honesty.

In a moment of complete vulnerability, her honesty captured my heart. At fifteen years of age I fell in love. I'm talking butterflies in my stomach, loss of appetite, type of love.

<u>*Proverbs 28:18 (ESV)*</u>
Whoever walks in integrity will be delivered,
but he who is crooked in his ways will
suddenly fall.

Although I wasn't sure how it would impact my future, I knew at that moment that this was "my girl". I knew that I had found my "good thing". Often in our pursuit to find success we overlook principles that have been designed to aid us in achieving our goals. I've come to realize that in the fall of 1985, classical music class 101, when I uttered the words, "look at the new girl", forever changed my destiny.

Hers

My destiny changed as well. All I could do was eat, sleep, think and dream about him. Constantly calling him on the phone and always wanting to be around him. I affectionately called him "Ricky" there was a song out called "Mickey", written by Toni Basil, so I would switch the words and say Ricky. The lyrics would say, Hey Ricky you so fine, you so fine you blow my mind Hey Ricky. As my husband stated earlier, we were destined to be together. The handsome young man that stood at the door of the music history class would forever change that new girl's life. I would have to say our souls met that day and we were headed for great things that we knew not of.

Romans 8:28 (KJV)
And we know that all things work together for good to them that love God, to them who are the called according to [his] purpose.

As you read this book and quote these scriptures from the Holy word of God, believe that your future is yet to be realized, lived and fulfilled.

Season... Time... Purpose

Ecclesiastes 3 1-17 (KJV)
To every thing there is a season, and a time to every purpose under the heaven: a time to be born, and a time to die; a time to plant, and a time to pluck up that which is planted; a time to kill, and a time to heal; a time to break down, and a time to build up; a time to weep, and a time to laugh; a time to mourn, and a time to dance; a time to cast away stones, and a time to gather stones together; a time to embrace, and a time to refrain from embracing; a time to get, and a time to lose; a time to

keep, and a time to cast away; a time to rend, and a time to sew; a time to keep silence, and a time to speak; a time to love, and a time to hate; a time of war, and a time of peace.

What profit hath he that worketh in that wherein he laboureth? I have seen the travail, which God hath given to the sons of men to be exercised in it. He hath made every thing beautiful in his time: also he hath set the world in their heart, so that no man can find out the work that God maketh from the beginning to the end. I know that there is no good in them, but for a man to rejoice, and to do good in his life. And also that every man should eat and drink, and enjoy the good of all his labour, it is the gift of God. I know that, whatsoever God doeth, it shall be for ever: nothing can be put to it, nor any thing taken from it: and God doeth it, that men should fear before him. That which hath been is now; and that which is to be hath already been; and God requireth that which is past.

And moreover I saw under the sun the place of judgment, that wickedness was there; and the place of righteousness, that iniquity was there. I said in mine heart, God shall judge the righteous and the wicked: for there is a time there for every purpose and for every work.

Chapter Two

Separation Anxiety

The High School Years

His

The early years of our relationship were full of passion, energy and reckless abandon. We loved, we argued, fought and cried together. Ultimately we became best friends. It would be those early years of passion, love and frustration that would develop us into who we are today. Was it easy? Not at all, It was possibly the most difficult and confusing time of our lives. We struggled to get to know each other, all while dealing with the nuances of peer pressure, high school, family and friends.

Again, we struggled, but we've come to realize that through it all, it was the will of God that we be together.

Scripture says:

John 6:37 (NIV)
All those the Father gives me will come to me, and whoever comes to me I will never drive away.

When God has a purpose for you, the enemy will do whatever he can to stop it! This is why you must endure trials, and trust in God! Remember, the Lord God Almighty has ordained your happiness; you just have to have confidence in a positive outcome to your situation.

Job 23:10 (KJV)
But he knoweth the way that I take: when he hath tried me, I shall come forth as gold.

Those early years were difficult because we were very young and confused. In addition to being immature, we had no examples of healthy love or mentors who believed in us as a couple. Essentially, we were on our own. However, God used this to develop a bond between us that has kept us together for 30 years! We had God ordained love for each other. The trials of life were purifying us. Even though there were times that "could have" destroyed our relationship, and bad decisions that "should have" destroyed us as a couple, God intervened and bestowed upon us, both Grace and Mercy.

Psalm 46:1 (NIV)
God is our refuge and strength, an ever-present help in trouble.

Needless to say, if it had not been for the Lord who was on our side, we wouldn't have made it. Together, we learned to fight every enemy that came our way. The enemies from outside, and the enemies within. Sometimes we fought obstacles with our backs against the wall, but we soon learned that we were more victorious fighting with our backs up against each other's. I had her back, she had mine, and the Lord covered us. We were only vulnerable when we were separated.

After two years of spending every opportunity to be with each other, we enrolled into different schools. It would be these years that would challenge our young love and raging hormones. Although she won't admit it, (LOL) I believe she was naughty as she found her independence. As for me, let's just say that I was messy. However, our love and passion wouldn't allow us to let go of each other. Therefore, the bond grew stronger. No matter who entered our lives, they were only temporary.

Hers

Although my husband thought I was naughty, I would have to say I was committed to our relationship hold heartedly. We had our ups and downs, but everybody knew that I was Ricky's Girl; Maybe I was naughty in the fact that I was stalking him (LOL), I was in Love. I am reminded of the story of Ruth and Boaz. My Boaz had found me and I accepted the assignment of this great appointment. I knew that God had ordained this union. My grandmother Lola Mae Jasper- Williams, (God rest her soul) had given her seal of approval just as Naomi had to Ruth. Our bond grew stronger and I believe the puzzle pieces were being fitly joined together. We were assigned to each other for "such a time as this".

Chapter Three

Married with Children

<u>Mark 10:9 (NIV)</u>
Therefore what God has joined together,
let no one separate.

His

After high school we began our family, and again we didn't have much support. We struggled in every aspect of our lives. It was as though we were being punished for choosing each other. Life was difficult and we often disagreed on everything. I was angry from sun up to sun down, always uptight and miserable. We were essentially alone; at least that's how I perceived things. However, as with all things we've discovered, the Lord used this time to teach us how to lean on, and have faith in, Him.

Hers

During this period of time I was extremely stressed out, being a new mother and a young bride. I had no idea what I had gotten myself into. I knew that I loved my husband and that I was in love with him, but we were not the 14 year olds meeting for the first time in that classical music class. This was the real world and it was different. I begin to seek God's face like never before. I knew that things had to change for the better. I remember having blue furniture, orange carpet and yellow curtains, (a decorators nightmare). I would sit in the middle of the floor of my living room and seek God's face. I prayed without ceasing.

1 Corinthians 7:14 (NIV)
**For the unbelieving husband has been
sanctified through his wife, and the
unbelieving wife has been sanctified through
her believing husband.
Otherwise your children would be unclean, but
as it is, they are holy.**

I would pray, not just for God to change him, I prayed that God would begin to change me and allow my husband to see God in me. My prayers were answered and my husband began to open before the Lord. We began reading the bible with each other, and when our oldest daughter was three months old, my husband came to church. He has been there from that day to this one. Our marriage began to be stronger. I watched my husband transform right before my eyes. I prayed for my husband to be saved not knowing that he would become a Bishop. A man of God, that the world needed to hear. I no longer leaned to my own understanding, I submitted to the Lord and our paths begin to shift.

His

I often wish that I had a father in my life that could've educated me on being a better husband to my young wife, and better father to my children. In addition to struggling financially, we had to learn not to allow our families to inject "their" drama into "our" lives. We actually discovered that our disagreements were more about other people's issues, than they were about ours. We had typical issues that young couples face, finances, raising our babies etc.. However, we allowed exterior conflict to invade our space. It took a few years for us to figure out that we were better off within our relationship when we excluded toxic people from it. It's painful when those that supposedly love you, constantly put you down.

Family members referred to our children as "stair step" children and "the less fortunate ones".

Again, it would take years to realize that these people and there toxic behavior wasn't welcomed nor needed in our lives. Although I've healed from those painful experiences, I recently had to encourage one of my children not to harbor ill feelings towards those whom they overheard utter such vitriol. I explained to them, that which I wish would have been done for me, and that's this, insecure and small minded people feel stronger bullying the vulnerable. Strong and secure people get no pleasure bullying, slandering or ostracizing those in need. Hopefully and prayerfully my advice is heeded so that the cycle and curse of anger is broken.

<u>*Proverbs 3:5-6 (NIV)*</u>
Trust in the Lord with all your heart
and lean not on your own understanding;
in all your ways submit to him,
and he will make your paths straight.

Chapter Four

Taming the Tongue

<u>James 3:1-12 (NIV)</u>

Not many of you should become teachers, my fellow believers, because you know that we who teach will be judged more strictly. We all stumble in many ways. Anyone who is never at fault in what they say is perfect, able to keep their whole body in check.

When we put bits into the mouths of horses to make them obey us, we can turn the whole animal. Or take ships as an example. Although they are so large and are driven by strong winds, they are steered by a very small rudder wherever the pilot wants to go.

Likewise, the tongue is a small part of the body, but it makes great boasts. Consider what a great forest is set on fire by a small spark. The tongue also is a fire, a world of evil among the parts of the body. It corrupts the whole body, sets the whole course of one's life on fire, and is itself set on fire by hell.

All kinds of animals, birds, reptiles and sea creatures are being tamed and have been tamed by mankind, but no human being can tame the tongue. It is a restless evil, full of deadly poison.
With the tongue we praise our Lord and Father, and with it we curse human beings, who have been made in God's likeness. Out of the same mouth come praise and cursing.

My brothers and sisters, this should not be. Can both fresh water and salt water flow from the same spring? My brothers and sisters, can a fig tree bear olives, or a grapevine bear figs? Neither can a salt spring produce fresh water.

His

We learned how to bond as a family; we gained strength from being ostracized. My wife is an exceptional mother. We affectionately referred to her back then as "the mama". She taught us how to love each other. I protected provided covered her and my children, and she nurtured, supported and prayed for our family. We learned how to survive together. As we are both hard workers, we developed as an effective team. She would work mornings and I would work afternoons. I had the children in the mornings, taking them to school and to daycare and she had the afternoon shift of feeding and leading. We worked together.

Hers

Despite the struggles we faced as a young couple, my husband had always demonstrated a strong work ethic. He was a great husband and a tremendous father, a good provider and a hard worker. It was those qualities and strengths that let me know that he would provide for our children and myself. Those attributes made me feel safe and secure. My husband was huge on being my protector. He would not let anyone use or abuse us even when it came down to family. He made it known not to disrespect him or his family.

The bible says in **1 Timothy 3:4,** *"He must manage his own family well and see that his children obey him, and he must do so in a manner worthy of full* *respect."* And he did just that, I believe that is why we bonded as a family, and gained strength.

Chapter Five

Socializing and Setting the Example

Proverbs 22:6 (NKJV)
Train up a child in the way he should go,
And when he is old he will not depart from it.

His

As I've previously stated, we have learned how to be an effective team, I have discovered that it's okay to make mistakes. I realize now, through trial and error, that love endures all things. I've heard the phrase uttered by other couples that "we're staying together for the sake of the kids". I must admit that our love and commitment to family played an intricate part in our staying married for quite a few years.

Children will challenge your very existence and have you question or examine every decision and every sacrifice that you've made concerning their life and yours. My knuckleheads definitely did just that, but I wouldn't change a thing.

Although raising a family is added pressure on a marriage, it would be our decision to dedicate our lives to Christ that would be the defining factor of change, stability and hope that would establish us as a healthy family. In 1993, Christ became the center of our lives and the anchor to our souls. We began to raise our children in the love and admonition of God. Again, our lives were changing. We became that young married Christian couple, with children. These years have proved to be the foundational years of the development of our faith in God and our trust in His love for our family.

Raising children challenges you on various levels, and we're still making adjustments. Earlier on I harbored serious resentment of the constant changes. It seemed as soon as we thought we had everything figured out, something would change. We had children, and each child has a different personality. However, training them in the principles of God was our focus, and keeping them safe from the streets and whiles of the devil was our objective. It has been a challenge to say the least, but a worthwhile one. We have accepted that change is constant an inevitable.

I joked once that I looked forward to the day when I could stop buying diapers and formula. I hadn't had a complete nights sleep in years. Well, our oldest is now married with three children of his own. Although I don't buy their diapers or formula, a good nights sleep still evades me. I say that because we're always covering them in prayer. We constantly cover all our children in prayer. Again, it's a life of adjustments, but a labor of love.

Hers

Our children were a glorious joy to our lives, and yes each of them had unique personalities to say the least. One child is very laid back, the other a jokester, one is very silly and the other very serious and the youngest is a mixture of them all. Watching them develop and grow up into upright young men and woman, who love the Lord, has been amazing. They are all saved and serving in the church, in some form or another. I am grateful that because of the way they were raised;

the streets were not able to get them. They are kingdom children, Glory to God.

To see my grandchildren growing up healthy and happy is delightful as well. Our son recently asked his dad the question, Dad how did you do it? How did you find the strength to discipline, instruct, train and raise us? Hearing my husband give him good godly advice warmed my heart. I must say many nights I prayed that God would allow our children to stay the course. I have to admit that I suffered anxiety separation when they began to move out on their own. I endured many sleepless nights, and I cried all the time. My husband would look at me and say its ok, to which I replied, honey, you just don't understand.

When the second oldest left the nest, I watched my husband go through like I did with the first. In order to cope with our children leaving the nest, my husband would transform their rooms as a project. He won't admit it but I know that's how he dealt with it. Raising our children has been a great honor, and I thank God everyday for entrusting me with such an assignment. They grow up so fast. My husband often jokes on how the older two were 16 and I still wanted to help them cross the street. God's word rings true, raise up a child in the way that is should go and when he is old he won't depart. They may stray from time to time, but they will always know to get back in place and on track. I am grateful for our children.

Chapter Six

When Loving You Is Hurting Me

<u>*John 3:16 (NIV)*</u>
> *For God so loved the world that he gave his one and only Son, that whoever believes in him shall not perish but have eternal life.*

Our deepest wounds have come from the people that we love the most; our most painful experiences have come from within the immediate family. Our trials, although ultimately beneficial have left deep wounds. What do you do when your enemy uses those you trust in an attempt to destroy all that you believe in, and all that you stand for?

<u>*Matthew 10:34-40 (KJV)*</u>
> *Think not that I am come to send peace on earth: I came not to send peace, but a sword.*

*For I am come to set a man at variance against
his father, and the daughter against her
mother, and the daughter in law against her
mother in law. And a man's foes shall be they
of his own household.*

*He that loveth father or mother more than me
is not worthy of me: and he that loveth son or
daughter more than me is not worthy of me.
And he that taketh not his cross, and
followeth after me, is not worthy of me.*

*He that findeth his life shall lose it: and he
that loseth his life for my sake shall find it.*

*He that receiveth you receiveth me, and he that
receiveth me receiveth him that sent me.*

Although we've suffered some devastating wounds, we must admit to administering a few of our own. However, through our love for our children and their love for us, we continually strive to uphold one another with love and forgiveness.

Matthew 6:14-15 NIV
*For if you forgive men when they sin against
you, your heavenly Father will also forgive
you. But if you do not forgive men their sins,
your Father will not forgive your sins.*

Colossians 3:13 NIV
**Bear with each other and forgive one another
if any of you has a grievance against someone.
Forgive as the Lord forgave you.**

We have learned that the sin of unforgiveness blocks
the flow of kingdom power. We have to exercise
forgiveness and at times that's easier said than done.
Boys become men and little girls grow up to become
women. We've learned to bury the past and heal from
the wounds of life's misunderstandings. Some things
were done out of immaturity and inexperience. Life
and its ups and downs, has to be lived one day and
one experience at a time.

Matthew 18:21-22 (NIV)
**Then Peter came to Jesus and asked, "Lord,
how many times shall I forgive my brother or
sister who sins against me? Up to seven
times?" Jesus answered, "I tell you, not seven
times, but seventy-seven times.**

Chapter Seven

The Process of Forgiveness

Because of our "open" wounds, we tend to "endure" life instead of living life. In order to live healthy we must heal from all of our painful and unpleasant experiences. That requires patience, time, counsel and sometimes therapy. While I'm discussing this particular subject, I must note that counsel and therapy, should be taken seriously. Seek qualified individuals in dealing with these matters, check their credentials. Someone with limited experience, or no experience at all concerning your issues is not necessarily the correct choice simply because they're your Pastors or leaders in your local church. I've sought counsel and therapy outside of the church on numerous occasions. Although I believe in the power to heal, I still seek the physician for medical advice. When in need of legal counsel, I seek an Attorney, and when I'm in need of restoration of my spirit, I seek the counsel of my Spiritual leaders. In order to heal from past and present wounds, you must do the following:

1. Forgive Yourself

Psalm 103:12 (NIV)
As far as the east is from the west, so far has he removed our transgressions from us.

2. Forgive God

Are you blaming God for things that have hurt you?

3. Forgive Your Family

Release Those Closest to You that may have hurt You

4. Forgive Others

Anyone that may have hurt you, (i.e - Church Hurts etc.)

Chapter Eight

Healing While Kneeling

<u>Psalm 86</u>
Hear me, Lord, and answer me,
for I am poor and needy.
Guard my life, for I am faithful to you;
save your servant who trusts in you.

You are my God; have mercy on me, Lord,
for I call to you all day long.
Bring joy to your servant, Lord,
for I put my trust in you.

You, Lord, are forgiving and good,
abounding in love to all who call to you.
Hear my prayer, Lord;
listen to my cry for mercy.

When I am in distress, I call to you,
because you answer me.

Among the gods there is none like you, Lord;
no deeds can compare with yours.

All the nations you have made
will come and worship before you, Lord;
they will bring glory to your name.

For you are great and do marvelous deeds;
you alone are God.

Teach me your way, Lord,
that I may rely on your faithfulness;
give me an undivided heart,
that I may fear your name.

I will praise you, Lord my God,
with all my heart;
I will glorify your name forever.
For great is your love toward me;
you have delivered me from the depths,
from the realm of the dead.

Arrogant foes are attacking me, O God;
ruthless people are trying to kill me —
they have no regard for you.

But you, Lord, are a compassionate
and gracious God, slow to anger,
abounding in love
and faithfulness.

Turn to me and have mercy on me;
show your strength in behalf of your servant;
save me, because I serve you
just as my mother did.

Give me a sign of your goodness,
that my enemies may see it and be put to
shame, for you, Lord, have helped me and
comforted me.

Pastor Tenisia's Personal Testimony

In the Fall of 2004, I was faced with the biggest trial of my life. In two months what started as minor discomfort, escalated into a full-blown attack that left the medical staff baffled. In just five months I lost 96lbs, had two surgeries, numerous biopsies and tests including a bone marrow harvesting. I lost my sense of smell, had pancreatitis and my gallbladder removed.

This disease was a mystery, threatened multiple organs including my lungs, eyes, heart and liver. Many names were called: Stroke, Bells Palsy, Cancer, Glaucoma, and Blindness, I went to numerous specialist: Ophthalmologists, Hematologists, Rheumatologists, and Pulmonologists. The diagnosis finally given was Sarcoidosis, but the Lord triumphed gloriously over them all!

In my time of sickness Love lifted me... As I reflect back during the time of my illness and how God used my husband, to pray me through this difficult time of affliction. It was a time in my life where I wanted to give up, quit, throw in the towel; I had a husband who would not let me go. It is true that the vows that we spoke   May 4, 1991 echoed in my ear "Till Death Do Us Part."

My husband spoke to death, starred it right in the face and spoke the word of God according to Isaiah 53:5 which reads:

> *But he was wounded for our transgressions, he*
> *was bruised for our iniquities: the*
> *chastisement of our peace was upon him; and*
> *with his stripes we are healed.*

She shall Live and not Die. When I did not have the strength to speak, eat, or hold my head up, because we were one flesh according to Mark 10:8, He began to speak Life so that I could be strengthened and lifted up before the Lord.

Mark 10:8
**And they twain shall be one flesh: so then they
are no more twain, but one flesh.**

Healing While Kneeling

Our story is one of faith, for when doctors declared that they'd done all that was medically possible and that I would die, I was sent home. My husband was instructed to keep me as comfortable as possible. However, my husband kept me in an environment of Praise, Prayer and worship: despite what the doctors had stated, He believed God. Who would have ever thought when I prayed my husband in to the kingdom year's prior, He would have to pray me through this difficult time in our lives. The strength of our faith and commitment to God was put to the test and triumphantly confirmed.

Deuteronomy 32:30
**How should one chase a thousand, and two
put ten thousand to flight, except their Rock
had sold them, and the Lord had shut them up?**

We began to speak the word of God and watch God manifest. The bible says in *Amos 3:3*, **"Can two walk**

together, except they be agreed?" *(KJV)* Our spirits began to come in agreement according to the word of God. We began to see Gods healing power manifested and I begin to get my strength back.

Now, I have my sense of smell and my strength, I can see not only in the natural but in the spirit. I am in my *Now*, preaching, teaching and sharing the word of the Lord. If God did it for me he can do it for you. It matters who you yoke up with. I thank God that in my time of need, *Love* truly lifted me. The Love that my husband has shown and shared towards me shall forever be in my heart.

Again, I thank God that he allowed me to meet my Husband in my freshman year of high school. I knew that he was the one the day our eyes locked in on each other. If Love has lifted me, I know it can lift you to.

<u>Proverbs 10:12 (KJV)</u>
Hatred stirreth up strifes: but love covereth all sins.

Chapter Nine

Surviving the Storm

Matthew 7:24-27 (NIV)
Therefore everyone who hears these words of mine and puts them into practice is like a wise man who built his house on the rock.

The rain came down, the streams rose, and the winds blew and beat against that house; yet it did not fall, because it had its foundation on the rock.

But everyone who hears these words of mine and does not put them into practice is like a foolish man who built his house on sand.

The rain came down, the streams rose, and the winds blew and beat against that house, and it fell with a great crash.

His

I believe that our commitment to each other was strengthened as a result of our trials. When we realized that each day could be our last it caused us to treat it as such. I certainly didn't want to lose my wife or my family. After all, she was my world, the mother of my children my partner in everything and best friend. Our bond is ridiculously strong. I joked once that I couldn't let her leave me with all these children. We no longer take each other for granted. Date night is a regular occurrence in our relationship. I don't wait for holidays to buy her gifts, because everyday is a gift from God.

Like wise, I encourage you to do the same. Appreciate the life that God has given you. Enjoy your spouse, your children and your family. We love, we laugh and we live, all to the glory of God! I can honestly say that I'm not only a blessed man; I'm a happy man.

The Lord has richly blessed us in many ways. Although we have a beautiful home and are no longer struggling as we did in those early years, what blesses me is the knowledge that I've gained from my experiences.

1. **I Know That God Loves Me**
2. **I Know That I Love God**
3. **I Love My Wife**
4. **I love My Children**
5. **I Love The Flock That I Shepherd**

Love Makes the Sacrifice

Throughout the years we have learned that life is a constant series of adjustments. Adjustments that we must be committed to adapting to.

It is the commitment to love that drives our ambition to diligently seek after the Lord, and what we believe to be *His* will concerning our lives. With every trial, we've confronted them head on with confidence that, through our faith in God and the power of love, we won't be defeated.

Over the years "Love" has demanded that we make concessions. We have learned the necessity of compromise, and the benefits of cooperation as it pertains to one another's needs.

We recognize the value of each other's presence, and we appreciate our individual contributions to the numerous relationships that we've formed:

God

Family

Church

Luke 10:27-28
> *And he answered, "YOU SHALL LOVE THE LORD YOUR GOD WITH ALL YOUR HEART, AND WITH ALL YOUR SOUL, AND WITH ALL YOUR STRENGTH, AND WITH ALL YOUR MIND; AND YOUR NEIGHBOR AS YOURSELF." And He said to him, "You have answered correctly; DO THIS AND YOU WILL LIVE." ...*

Matthew 6:33 (KJV)
> *But seek ye first the kingdom of God, and his righteousness; and all these things shall be added unto you.*

It is our continued prayer that Gods love lifts you.

1 Thessalonians 3:12(KJV)
> *And the Lord make you to increase and abound in love one toward another, and toward all men, even as we do toward you:*

WE LOVE YOU, LOVE YOU, LOVE YOU

To Be Continued...

Divine Restoration Ministries
DRMMinistries.org

Detroit Campus
16392 Harper Avenue, Detroit, MI 48224
(313) 884-5365 Phone • (831) 887-5365 Fax
Email: divine@drmministries.org
Toll Free: (877) APOSTL-7

Tune Into
Restoration Today
With
Bishop J. Richard & Prophetess Tenisia Evans

The Impact Network: Friday, 8:00 AM
You can also watch Restoration Today online
at:
The Impact Network

Comcast: Friday, 8:00 AM Ch. 400

Dish Network: Ch. 268
Sunday, 8:00 AM